Second Corinthians

Bart Adkins

Copyright 2016 by Bart Adkins.
The book author retains sole copyright to
his contributions to this book.
Published 2016.
Printed in the United States of America.

All rights reserved.

No portion of this book may be reproduced, stored in a retrieval system, or transmitted in any form or by any means – electronic, mechanical, photocopy, recording, scanning, or other – except for brief quotations in critical reviews or articles, without the prior written permission of the author.

ISBN 978-1-946234-03-2

Front cover design by Mark Gauthier.

This book was published by BookCrafters,
Parker, Colorado.
bookcrafterscolorado@gmail.com

This book may be ordered from
www.bookcrafters.net and other online bookstores.

Foreword

Thank you for selecting this volume of the Expository series. These volumes are the contribution of various Apostolic writers. Their biography is on the back cover. The publishers of the Expository series would like to extend a thank you for helping us get this valuable material into the hands of readers.

The desire is that people would read the scriptures and be blessed. These commentary works, or works of Expository subjects, will give insight to, and further the understanding of the readers.

Each of these authors hold the values of the original Apostles of Jesus Christ. These writers want to hold to the values expostulated in the New Testament by Jesus and his disciples. Each of them ascribe to the concept offered by the Apostle John, "I have no greater joy than to hear that my children walk in truth."

Truth has been passed down through generations and has survived critics and doubters. Truth will prevail and ultimately triumph.

These writings are our contribution to the river of written truth that has flowed down through the ages.

Read and be blessed.

Kenneth Bow

Introduction

There is little debate that it was probably the Corinthian church that caused Paul more heartache than any other of the churches over which he had authority. Indeed, the language of correspondence in Paul's letters, both the first and second, testifies to the profound gravity of circumstances prevalent in Corinth.

It was a prosperous, commercial port city, the capital of the Achaian province, and a thriving Roman colony. Corinth was at the heart of world trade and a menagerie of cultural backgrounds including Romans, Greeks, those from the Far East, and Jews. Corinth's reputation for an undisguised immorality had been earned in the early days of the old city. Long had the term "Corinthianize" been coined as a euphemism for fornication, and a "Corinthian girl" was known to be a harlot. It was said that the temple of Aphrodite was, at all times, staffed by a thousand of them. Against this backdrop we find Paul again addressing the needs of a church surrounded by a deplorable state of depravity.

Written sometime after in late 56 or 57 AD, Paul composed 2 Corinthians while in Macedonia, expressing both a sincere exuberance and relief at their repentance before God and for their reunion to his guidance. Nevertheless there was a faction still in opposition to his leadership and he writes to clear his name of their false charges and to implore that a Godly sorrow might be found in these dissidents before he came to Corinth once again.

While there is no single, unifying theme for the book, the overarching tone is one of deliberate reflection of the church as a whole, it's highs and lows, its purpose, and ultimate direction. The driving message that pervades the entire letter is one defending the sincerity and authority of God called ministry, and a call to genuine, reflective repentance. Within its pages Paul covers much ground including a clarification of misunderstandings, his feelings regarding the conduct of the church and his reprimand, the moral fiber of a Christian minster, his joy over their reunification, a reminder of collections for Jerusalem, a defense to his detractors, the proof of apostolic calling, a call and admonition towards self control, and his heartfelt prayer for their success.

Chapter 1

1.1-2 Paul, an apostle of Jesus Christ by the will of God, and Timothy our brother, unto the church of God which is at Corinth, with all the saints which are in all Achaia: 2 Grace be to you and peace from God our Father, and from the Lord Jesus Christ.

1.1-2 In standard fashion Paul begins with a salutation to his intended audience. As if to remind the Corinthian church, Paul states that his apostleship is not in question but is in accord with the "will of God." While such language would not be atypical of Paul, this particular occasion has an added significance in light of the recent challenge to his calling and leadership. In a manner akin to acknowledging joint authorship Paul references Timothy, his "son in the faith" (1 Tim. 1:2), here calling him "brother," perhaps a reference to their maturing relationship or of Timothy's increased responsibilities among the various assemblies. Despite the obvious struggles at Corinth Paul still believes them to be God's elect, the saints, remembering the Lord's words that He had "much people in this city." (Acts 18:10) Writing to "all the saints in all Achaia" one can see strong evidence that, though aimed specifically at Corinth's issues, this letter may well have been read aloud each of the region's established churches.

1.3-7 Blessed be God, even the Father of our Lord Jesus Christ, the Father of mercies, and the God of all comfort; 4 Who comforteth us in all our tribulation, that we may be able to comfort them which are in any trouble, by the comfort wherewith we ourselves are comforted of God. 5 For as the sufferings of Christ abound in us, so our consolation also aboundeth by Christ. 6 And whether we be afflicted, it is for your consolation and salvation, which is effectual in the enduring of the same sufferings which we also suffer: or whether we be comforted, it is for your consolation and salvation. 7 And our hope of you is stedfast, knowing, that as ye are partakers of the sufferings, so shall ye be also of the consolation.

1.3-7 Paul understood the paradox in the core meaning of grace for, though it be loved by all the church, it is best experienced by those enduring the worst of times. The tribulations here mentioned is the Greek "thlipsis," meaning trouble, pressure, and distress; Paul references this word nine times throughout this second letter to Corinth. If anyone knew trouble and hardship, it was Paul, but it is specifically in this trouble that the blessing and consolation of God is most vividly recognized. (Not surprisingly, the "comfort" Paul mentions is the Greek parakaleo, another form of that invoked in John 14:16, 26, parakletos, in relation to the Holy Ghost.) It is directly through, not around, the affliction that His people work towards their "consolation and salvation." The believer is to remember that if one is to go through the trial, one must and will receive the relief of His Comforter.

1.8-11 For we would not, brethren, have you ignorant of our trouble which came to us in Asia, that we were pressed out of measure, above strength, insomuch that we despaired even of life: 9 But we had the sentence of death in ourselves, that we should not trust in ourselves, but in God which raiseth the dead: 10 Who delivered us from so great a death, and doth deliver: in whom we trust that he will yet deliver us; 11 Ye also helping together by prayer for us, that for the gift bestowed upon us by the means of many persons thanks may be given by many on our behalf.

1.8-11 While the Corinthians may have been aware of the hardship which had befallen Paul in Asia, perhaps communicated to them by the mouth of Titus, they were undeniably unaware of it's severity. Rather than camouflage his true feelings the apostle chooses to elaborate on the state of affairs and how low the trial had brought him. The trouble (thlipsis), whatever it may have been, was of such grave concern that Paul doubted he would get out alive. He had fully expected death, but rather than trying to illicit sympathy or stir emotion, Paul takes occasion to retell the story as a means to reinforce a principle. It will not be by the might or power of mankind (Zec. 14:6) that deliverance comes, but by His Spirit through the "effectual fervent prayer" (James 5:16) of the saints.

1.12 For our rejoicing is this, the testimony of our conscience, that in simplicity and godly sincerity, not with fleshly wisdom, but by the grace of God, we have had our conversation in the world, and more abundantly to you-ward.

1.12 Paul meets the dispute over his motives directly. He states assertively, and in no uncertain language, that the rationale behind all his conduct regarding the church has been in "simplicity" (Greek "haplotes," single-mindedness, directed), was done with all sincerity, and through the grace of God, not according to the wisdom or reasoning of a fleshly world.

1.13-14 For we write none other things unto you, than what ye read or acknowledge; and I trust ye shall acknowledge even to the end; 14 As also ye have acknowledged us in part, that we are your rejoicing, even as ye also are our's in the day of the Lord Jesus.

1.13-14 All of his communications with the Corinthians have been straightforward; there has been no hidden agenda or need to reading between the lines. The man of God makes prayer for hindsight, a hope that, one day, the church may look back and be proud of Paul's conscientious and principled teaching.

1.15-16 And in this confidence I was minded to come unto you before, that ye might have a second benefit; 16 And to pass by you into Macedonia, and to come again out of Macedonia unto you, and of you to be brought on my way toward Judaea.

1.15-16 With the confidence of his strong connection to the church, Paul's original intention had been a journey from Ephesus allowing him to visit the Corinthian's twice, the "second benefit." His initial design was one bourn out of a love for Corinth and the desire to be with them as often as he could.

1.17-18 When I therefore was thus minded, did I use lightness? or the things that I purpose, do I purpose according to the flesh, that with me there should be yea yea, and nay nay? 18 But as God is true, our word toward you was not yea and nay.

1.17-18 His defense continues with the attestation that the decision to change plans was not one made lightly. While his opponents claimed his actions proved an indecisive unreliability, Paul argues that it was not done "according to the flesh" (selfishly motivated), not like those of the world who say "yes" but really mean "no."

1.19-20 For the Son of God, Jesus Christ, who was preached among you by us, even by me and Silvanus and Timotheus, was not yea and nay, but in him was yea. 20 For all the promises of God in him are yea, and in him Amen, unto the glory of God by us.

1.19-20 The stability alluded to is that of God Himself. It was the message of the Christ which Paul, Silas, and Timothy had preached to them. Though the power of the Lord's Word, when God says yes, it is done; there is no wavering, and "one jot or one tittle shall in no wise pass from the law" (Matt. 5:18) until the entirety of His Word is accomplished. The only acceptable answer to His Word is "amen"!

1.21-22 Now he which stablisheth us with you in Christ, and hath anointed us, is God; 22 Who hath also sealed us, and given the earnest of the Spirit in our hearts.

1.21-22 It is God alone who has established the church

and anointed His chosen apostles; it is through Him only that His people are enabled to stand firm. Those who have been "sealed" (Greek "sphragizo," stamped with approval) with the Holy Ghost have been given the "earnest" (Greek "arrabon," a pledge or down payment) on the inheritance (Eph. 1:14) which is to come.

1.23-24 Moreover I call God for a record upon my soul, that to spare you I came not as yet unto Corinth. 24 Not for that we have dominion over your faith, but are helpers of your joy: for by faith ye stand.

1.23-24 Paul's change in plans had obviously caused no small amount of confusion in confidence as is attested by the powerful language he invokes by calling "God for a record" or, as his witness to the stand. Paul now tells the whole story, the true reason for his departure from original plans; it was an act of mercy to spare the Corinthians a vehement rebuke in the heat of the moment. Paul, like so many of us, needed time to cool off. He asserts that it will not be by domination of their actions, living their lives for them, that any would make it, but that all who stand in faith will do so in the bond of unity; Paul needs Corinth; Corinth needs Paul.

Chapter 2

2.1-2 But I determined this with myself, that I would not come again to you in heaviness. 2 For if I make you sorry, who is he then that maketh me glad, but the same which is made sorry by me?

2.1-2 The apostle substantiates his absence with the reasoning that he grated reprieve from a further painful visit. He wished not to bring "heaviness" (Greek "lype," grief) for if he caused them sorrow who would make them glad?

2.3-4 And I wrote this same unto you, lest, when I came, I should have sorrow from them of whom I ought to rejoice; having confidence in you all, that my joy is the joy of you all. 4 For out of much affliction and anguish of heart I wrote unto you with many tears; not that ye should be grieved, but that ye might know the love which I have more abundantly unto you.

2.3-4 The letter to the Corinthians was thus sent in lieu of him so that, when he arrived in person, he might not be grieved by those who ought to bring joy. He is confident in his conviction that his joy could deb theirs also. He affirms that it was in much "anguish" (Greek "synoche," distress & anxiety) that he wrote to them with tears; it was not done to injure but, rather, to show the extreme of his love and care for their future wellbeing.

2.5-8 But if any have caused grief, he hath not grieved me, but in part: that I may not overcharge you all. 6 Sufficient to such a man is this punishment, which was inflicted of many. 7 So that contrariwise ye ought rather to forgive him, and comfort him, lest perhaps such a one should be swallowed up with overmuch sorrow. 8 Wherefore I beseech you that ye would confirm your love toward him.

2.5-8 What event made the visit a painful one is unknown, however, the provocation for the severe letter seems to have been centered around the actions of one man. While Paul does identify with a personal hurt, he does not presuppose that the whole church was not adversely affected also. While the majority opposed him and, to some degree dispensed punishment, Paul now defends his detractor on the grounds that Corinth may go to far in oppressing him. The time to forgive has come lest the man be swallowed up in discouragement.

2.9-11 For to this end also did I write, that I might know the proof of you, whether ye be obedient in all things. 10 To whom ye forgive any thing, I forgive also: for if I forgave any thing, to whom I forgave it, for your sakes forgave I it in the person of Christ; 11 Lest Satan should get an advantage of us: for we are not ignorant of his devices.

2.9-11 Paul's purpose in writing the letter was not only one of personal vindication but to "know the proof" of the people, to test their obedience God's law and demonstrate the level of commitment they had towards their pastor. Because of their solidarity with Paul, as one, they would forgive the man who had wrong them by wronging Paul. Otherwise, Satan would "get an advantage of" them all but, because Paul and Corinth are "not ignorant of his devices," the root of bitterness (Heb. 12:5) could not spring up.

2.12-13 Furthermore, when I came to Troas to preach Christ's gospel, and a door was opened unto me of the Lord, 13 I had no rest in my spirit, because I found not Titus my brother: but taking my leave of them, I went from thence into Macedonia.

2.12-13 Arriving in Troas with a divinely inspired "open door" to preach the word, Paul could not accomplish the work with any sense of peace because Titus had not yet arrived with news of Corinth's situation. Leaving Troas, Paul set his sights on Macedonia, in search on Titus, and in the hope of good news from Corinth.

2.14-17 Now thanks be unto God, which always causeth us to triumph in Christ, and maketh manifest the savour of his knowledge by us in every place. 15 For we are unto God a sweet savour of Christ, in them that are saved, and in them that perish: 16 To the one we are the savour of death unto death; and to the other the savour of life unto life. And who is sufficient for these things? 17 For we are not as many, which corrupt the word of God: but as of sincerity, but as of God, in the sight of God speak we in Christ.

2.14-17 Paul thanks God, who knows exactly what He is doing and, though he or anyone of the church end up in situations they had not counted on, the Lord allows the "savour" (Greek "osme," aroma) of His sweet perfume to be spread in all these places. Paul compares the Message to that of a fragrance; for those seeking life and God's way it is a sweet smelling bouquet of life. But, to those seeking their own way, the way that seems right to them (Prov. 14:12), the Message is one of doom. Who among God's church is worthy for such a task? God's chosen do not spread His Word out of a desire to please mankind or market Him for profit, but it is done in grave sincerity, with the knowledge that He is watching us.

Chapter 3

3.1-3 Do we begin again to commend ourselves? or need we, as some others, epistles of commendation to you, or letters of commendation from you? 2 Ye are our epistle written in our hearts, known and read of all men: 3 Forasmuch as ye are manifestly declared to be the epistle of Christ ministered by us, written not with ink, but with the Spirit of the living God; not in tables of stone, but in fleshy tables of the heart.

3.1-3 A common practice of Paul's day was for a traveler, in whatever business they might be employed, to carry letters of recommendation; the apostle himself al practiced this method of endorsement from time to time (Rom. 16:1-2; 2 Cor. 8:22-24). This would serve to validate the traveler's claims in far reaching areas where their skills and credentials might be in doubt or their motives suspect. Paul's first question ("Do we begin again to commend ourselves"?) immediately gives the impression that there were some in Corinth carrying their owns letters, perhaps some of questionable authenticity, and that this was not the first time such self-proclamation had gone on in the church. And while their letters might not have been made readily available for general validation, Paul says clearly that he needs no such letter. Rather, the only letter he needs here is the Corinthians themselves ("Ye are our epistle…"); this letter was ready for open examination by anyone who wished to study it ("…known and read of all men:"). This letter of the soul stands in stark contrast to that of human wisdom chiseled in stone, for this letter is written by the Holy Ghost directly upon the heart.

3.4-6 And such trust have we through Christ to Godward: 5 Not that we are sufficient of ourselves to think any thing as of ourselves; but our sufficiency is of God; 6 Who also hath made us able ministers of the new testament; not of the letter, but of the spirit: for the letter killeth, but the spirit giveth life.

3.4-6 Paul desires to convince the Corinthians, at the heart of a civilized world bowing before human achievement, that his confidence in them does not lie in their own ability but in the power of God within them. Furthermore, Paul, and his fellow workers, have not been established by any innate "sufficiency" but established to do the work thru the qualifications given by the Holy Ghost. They have been enabled (1 Tim. 1:12) to preach a message of the heart, not of laws, bringing life in place of death.

3.7-12 But if the ministration of death, written and engraven in stones, was glorious, so that the children of Israel could not stedfastly behold the face of Moses for the glory of his countenance; which glory was to be done away: 8 How shall not the ministration of the spirit be rather glorious? 9 For if the ministration of condemnation be glory, much more doth the ministration of righteousness exceed in glory. 10 For

even that which was made glorious had no glory in this respect, by reason of the glory that excelleth. 11 For if that which is done away was glorious, much more that which remaineth is glorious. 12 Seeing then that we have such hope, we use great plainness of speech:

3.7-12 The apostle writes here of the sharply defined disparity of the Old and New Covenants. This may imply that his opponents, those sporting their own "letters," might have themselves been harboring the old rather than welcoming the new. Paul here begins with an explanation that the New Covenant is not superior, rather, more easily approached by flawed humanity. The Law, etched in stone, was "glorious," glorious enough to make the face of Moses literally shine with it's writing, so magnificent, though, that mere flesh could not aspire to it's grandeur; the Lord, though, has promised something new (Jer. 31:31-34). Again, the distinction is presented; the Law in all of it's glory could only end in death, but the cross, as ultimate fulfillment of the Old, brings everlasting life. While the Old covenant was "glorious" (Greek "doxazo," honored, magnified) the New "excelleth" (Greek "hyperballo" exceeds, surpasses) in it's ability to transpose finite flesh into immortality. It is because of this excellence that His people, in the courage of His overcoming, might have "plainness of speech," a life of Holy Ghost boldness! (Heb. 4:16)

3.13-16 And not as Moses, which put a veil over his face, that the children of Israel could not stedfastly look to the end of that which is abolished: 14 But their minds were blinded: for until this day remaineth the same vail untaken away in the reading of the old

testament; which vail is done away in Christ. 15 But even unto this day, when Moses is read, the vail is upon their heart. 16 Nevertheless when it shall turn to the Lord, the vail shall be taken away.

3.13-16 We do not try to cover up the glory, as was the case with Moses' face, veiled from a people whose hearts were hardened, not ready to experience the fullness of the Lord's brightness. Whatever Moses' original purpose in donning the veil, it proved to be prophetic. (Ex. 34:35) Both Israel of that day, and many of the Jews of Paul's day (even to the present) refused to perceive that the Old Covenant was only the first part of God's ultimate Message to mankind. As Paul so aptly taught the Corinthians, it is only the revelation of the Mighty God in Christ (Col. 2:9), not a replaced covenant but a fulfilled one, that can rend the veil (Matt. 27:51) and allow mankind see the brightness of His Glory, Jesus, the express image of His person! (Heb. 1:3)

3.17-18 Now the Lord is that Spirit: and where the Spirit of the Lord is, there is liberty. 18 But we all, with open face beholding as in a glass the glory of the Lord, are changed into the same image from glory to glory, even as by the Spirit of the Lord.

3.17-18 Again attesting to the fullness of the Godhead in Christ, Paul instructs the church that the Lord (Jesus) "is that Spirit" (the Holy Ghost). The product of His presence with people, Emmanuel, is freedom; redeemed from under the Law, the church is "no more a servant" (Gal. 4:5-7) but made heirs to the promise of liberty. Those filled with the Holy Ghost, those for whom the curtain on the stage of time has been lifted, can see His glory clearer from day to day, having their image "changed" (Greek "metamorphoo," transformed; as in Rom. 12:2) to be a reflection of His singular magnificence. (See also Eph. 4:23-24)

Chapter 4

4.1 Therefore seeing we have this ministry, as we have received mercy, we faint not;

4.1 There can be no ministry without mercy, and only through that mercy can one minister faithfully until the end. Though the minister suffer discouragement, and feel as if to "faint" (Greek "ekkakeo," be weary, lose heart), the decision to continue, to never give up, will reap the harvest of saving grace. (Gal. 6:9; Matt. 24:13)

4.2 But have renounced the hidden things of dishonesty, not walking in craftiness, nor handling the word of God deceitfully; but by manifestation of the truth commending ourselves to every man's conscience in the sight of God.

4.2 Surely a great source of discouragement for Paul was the continual stirring of false prophets in Corinth; these incited doubt within the core church, which should have trusted Paul implicitly. It was the actions of these to which Paul refers when he references "hidden things," "craftiness," and use of God's Word "deceitfully" and, indeed, in dealing with them takes up a major portion of this letter's content. Paul's reaction is one of unashamed opposition to these unaddressed, secret agendas on the grounds that he and his spokesmen have only ever spoken in plain, honest truth.

4.3-4 But if our gospel be hid, it is hid to them that are lost: 4 In whom the god of this world hath blinded the minds of them which believe not, lest the light of the glorious gospel of Christ, who is the image of God, should shine unto them.

4.3-4 For so many of Paul's day, and countless generations after, they could not receive the things of the Spirit of God (1 Cor. 2:14), the full scope of the message being preached. The prince and power of the air (Eph. 2:2),the rulers of the darkness of this world (Eph. 6:12), had already blinded many eyes.

4.5 For we preach not ourselves, but Christ Jesus the Lord; and ourselves your servants for Jesus' sake.

4.5 Speaking to the fact that the Gospel is meant to have one boast only, Paul's words are reminiscent of his first letter to the Corinthians that he was resolute in his decision to know nothing else "except Jesus Christ and him crucified." (1 Cor. 2:2)

4.6-7 For God, who commanded the light to shine out of darkness, hath shined in our hearts, to give the light of the knowledge of the glory of God in the face of Jesus Christ. 7 But we have this treasure in earthen vessels, that the excellency of the power may be of God, and not of us.

4.6-7 The same God who, in the beginning said "let there be light" (Gen. 1:3), is the God of all flesh (Jer.

32:27) who has placed that same marvelous light (1 Pet. 2:9) in our hearts, a gift to those who sit in darkness (Lu. 1:78-79). In comparison to any pastor who could have written to the Corinthian church, Paul had a special appreciation for the knee-bending power of the light of God, Heavenly illumination that changed his life on the road to Damascus. (Ac. 9:3-9)

4.8-9 We are troubled on every side, yet not distressed; we are perplexed, but not in despair; 9 Persecuted, but not forsaken; cast down, but not destroyed;

4.8-9 These Pauline paradoxes are well known in the circles of Christian exegesis. While applicable to a broad swath of daily living, specifically for Paul it is significant that, were it not for God's grace, the these troublesome moments in Corinth's history would have likely broken him. It is notable that the use of "perplexed" (Greek "aporeo," desparing, no way out) and "in despair" (Greek "exaporeo," utterly at a loss, totally despairing) are similar words emphasizing the same point; the emotions and hurts were nagging to the point of giving up. In the struggles of life these feelings are nothing new for the modern Apostolic. God provided the courage then, for Paul was not destroyed, and the Lord will *never* forsake His people. (Deut. 31:6)

4.10-12 Always bearing about in the body the dying of the Lord Jesus, that the life also of Jesus might be made manifest in our body. 11 For we which live are always delivered unto death for Jesus' sake, that the life also of Jesus might be made manifest in our mortal flesh. 12 So then death worketh in us, but life in you.

4.10-12 Quite literally for the Christians living in Corinth, their religious freedom and, to a great extent, their very lives, existed at the whim of the Roman empire. It was not uncommon for Christians of that day to suffer physical beatings, imprisonments, and the possibility of being used as lion fodder for the sake of the coliseum's games. Paul compares their daily sufferings or persecutions to sharing in the death of Christ, a comparison Jesus himself had made and one that Paul would have been keenly aware of. (Matt. 5:10-12)

4.13-15 We having the same spirit of faith, according as it is written, I believed, and therefore have I spoken; we also believe, and therefore speak; 14 Knowing that he which raised up the Lord Jesus shall raise up us also by Jesus, and shall present us with you. 15 For all things are for your sakes, that the abundant grace might through the thanksgiving of many redound to the glory of God.

4.13-15 As Abraham believed God and righteousness was found in him (Gen. 15:6; Rom. 4:3), and as the psalmist was also convinced (Ps. 116:10), to be thoroughly persuaded of His unlimited ability is to find victory to speak and live the truth. To take heed in the doctrine and commitment to his way (1 Tim. 4:16) is to pere abundant grace to all that will hear the Word.

4.16-18 For which cause we faint not; but though our outward man perish, yet the inward man is renewed day by day. 17 For our light affliction, which is but for a moment, worketh for us a far more exceeding and eternal weight of glory; 18 While we look not at

the things which are seen, but at the things which are not seen: for the things which are seen are temporal; but the things which are not seen are eternal.

4.16-18 Here the things seen, the things that are temporal, are analogous to the profit of one seeking the gain of this world to the losing of his soul (Mark 8:36-37). Paul preached a similar message to the church in Rome (Rom. 8:18) advising the congregation not to compare the sufferings of this life with what God would reveal. What the church may encounter on a daily basis is sometimes the trying fire (1 Pet. 1:6-7) necessary to separate the pure gold of faith from the dross of the Great Refiner's ultimate work. (See also Job 23:10)

Chapter 5

5.1-10 For we know that if our earthly house of this tabernacle were dissolved, we have a building of God, an house not made with hands, eternal in the heavens. 2 For in this we groan, earnestly desiring to be clothed upon with our house which is from heaven: 3 If so be that being clothed we shall not be found naked. 4 For we that are in this tabernacle do groan, being burdened: not for that we would be unclothed, but clothed upon, that mortality might be swallowed up of life. 5 Now he that hath wrought us for the selfsame thing is God, who also hath given unto us the earnest of the Spirit. 6 Therefore we are always confident, knowing that, whilst we are at home in the body, we are absent from the Lord: 7 (For we walk by faith, not by sight:) 8 We are confident, I say, and willing rather to be absent from the body, and to be present with the Lord. 9 Wherefore we labour, that, whether present or absent, we may be accepted of him. 10 For we must all appear before the judgment seat of Christ; that every one may receive the things done in his body, according to that he hath done, whether it be good or bad.

5.1-10 As is often the case, with the addition of chapter

and verse divisions ex post facto (to what was almost certainly intended to be long prose), continuity can easily be lost. The division between chapters 4 and 5 is one such, unfortunate case; what Paul begins to set forth in the first 10 verses of chapter 5 relies exclusively on a firm grounding on the antithesis of temporary and eternal set down in the closing of chapter 4. Indeed, speaking of clothing, groaning, and burdens of bodies, one might be quick to surmise that Paul is hemmed up in mortal woes. However, the "tabernacle" (Greek "skenos," temporary residence, human body) of which Paul speaks must be understood in the light of the "building from God, an eternal house in heaven, not built by human hands"; the wording is reminiscent of the Lord's explanation of His own resurrected self, a temple "made without hands." (Mark 14:58) Paul seeks to convey a message to his listeners that, while we are here in this world, though there may be gain or loss, the ultimate prize and high calling (Phi. 3:14) of Christ is not on earth, but treasure in heaven. (Matt. 6:19-21) The walk of God's people is not achieved by "sight" (Greek "eidos," appearance, fashion, form) but it is one of "faith" (Greek "pistis," assurance, persuasion) in things the Lord has prepared that the "eye hath not seen." (Isa. 64:4) Paul's assertion, "rather to be absent from the body," is a solemn protest against all things carnal. He would choose, rather, to opt out of the flesh and stand, pleasing, before God in judgment. Pleasing Him, being with Him, is of ultimate concern; we are reminded of the words of the Revelator, "…Even so, come, Lord Jesus." (Rev. 22:20)

5.11-15 Knowing therefore the terror of the Lord, we persuade men; but we are made manifest unto God; and I trust also are made manifest in your consciences.

12 For we commend not ourselves again unto you, but give you occasion to glory on our behalf, that ye may have somewhat to answer them which glory in appearance, and not in heart. 13 For whether we be beside ourselves, it is to God: or whether we be sober, it is for your cause. 14 For the love of Christ constraineth us; because we thus judge, that if one died for all, then were all dead: 15 And that he died for all, that they which live should not henceforth live unto themselves, but unto him which died for them, and rose again.

5.11-15 Herein lies the culmination of the Great Commission for, in the fear of God, the apostle and his brethren are persuaders of men. Paul was not unaccustomed of being thought mad (Acts. 26:24), but for one consumed by doing all things through the mind of Christ (Phil. 2:5-8), it is the mad, unbridled love of Christ, which "constraineth" (Greek "synecho," holds, controls) our thinking and actions.

5.16-17 Wherefore henceforth know we no man after the flesh: yea, though we have known Christ after the flesh, yet now henceforth know we him no more. 17 Therefore if any man be in Christ, he is a new creature: old things are passed away; behold, all things are become new.

5.16-17 This new thinking will, at the same time, direct our sight towards others. The mind's eye of the Holy Ghost cannot evaluate mankind according to the view of the flesh, for He alone searches the heart and tries the reigns. (Jer. 17:10) For the one who is in Christ, the "old man" is crucified and buried with Him (Rom. 6:6; Eph. 4:22; Col. 3:9); we are resurrected into "newness of life"

(Rom. 6:4) and the former "ways of death" pass away. (Prov. 16:25; Rom. 5:21

5.18-19 And all things are of God, who hath reconciled us to himself by Jesus Christ, and hath given to us the ministry of reconciliation; 19 To wit, that God was in Christ, reconciling the world unto himself, not imputing their trespasses unto them; and hath committed unto us the word of reconciliation.

5.18-19 With His sacrifice the Lord has "reconciled" (Greek, "katallasso," to change mutually) the world unto Himself, becoming flesh to die so that we might gain the Spirit to live! The elucidation of reconciliation, as to it's defining qualities, brings newfound appreciation for the work of the Cross; to reconcile is to restore, to win over, make compatible, and bring into harmony and agreement. The New Covenant in the heart of man has granted accord with the law of God.

5.20-21 Now then we are ambassadors for Christ, as though God did beseech you by us: we pray you in Christ's stead, be ye reconciled to God. 21 For he hath made him to be sin for us, who knew no sin; that we might be made the righteousness of God in him.

5.20-21 As the emissary of Heaven, the delegation sent by God to a dying world, the Church stands strong. It is built on the foundation of the apostles and prophets (Eph. 2:20) and its unshakable cornerstone is God in flesh. The Church is that city set on a hill (Matt. 5:14), representatives of Calvary, appointed witnesses of light to a world of darkness. (Isa. 43:10; Matt. 28:19)

Chapter 6

6.1-2 We then, as workers together with him, beseech you also that ye receive not the grace of God in vain. 2 (For he saith, I have heard thee in a time accepted, and in the day of salvation have I succoured thee: behold, now is the accepted time; behold, now is the day of salvation.)

6.1-2 The words of Paul call to mind God's commandment that "Thou shalt not take the name of the LORD thy God in vain...." For to be baptized in His name, to be filled with His Spirit and continue in our old ways of living, is the greatest ineffectual manipulation of His blood that man could decline to; God forbid. (Rom. 6:1) There were obviously false prophets in Corinth teaching a message contrary to that of the Cross (2. Cor. 11:4); these were, to be sure, taking the Gospel of the Christ "in vain." It is then interesting that Paul quotes Isaiah 49:8 as a rebuttal to those Judaizers who would have imposed Mosaic Law as the sole means of salvation; furthermore, not only would salvation be available to Israel, but alto the Gentiles at large. (Isa. 49:9)

6.3-10 Giving no offence in any thing, that the

ministry be not blamed: 4 But in all things approving ourselves as the ministers of God, in much patience, in afflictions, in necessities, in distresses, 5 In stripes, in imprisonments, in tumults, in labours, in watchings, in fastings; 6 By pureness, by knowledge, by long suffering, by kindness, by the Holy Ghost, by love unfeigned, 7 By the word of truth, by the power of God, by the armour of righteousness on the right hand and on the left, 8 By honour and dishonour, by evil report and good report: as deceivers, and yet true; 9 As unknown, and yet well known; as dying, and, behold, we live; as chastened, and not killed; 10 As sorrowful, yet alway rejoicing; as poor, yet making many rich; as having nothing, and yet possessing all things.

6.3-10 Here waxing poetic, Paul covers every possible contingency the struggling child of God might encounter on this Christian journey. It is captivating to realize that, in all these situations where children of God can be "more than conquerors" (Rom. 8:35-39), Paul makes it abundantly clear that the weight of responsibility to give no "offense" (Greek, "proskope," occasion to sin) lies squarely on the shoulders of the believer. It is incumbent upon the Church that we provide no cause for failure or misstep to any we cross paths with, no matter what predicament we might be in. When the weight of the world is upon our shoulders, we must stand in grace so as not to become a stumbling block for others.

6.11-13 O ye Corinthians, our mouth is open unto you, our heart is enlarged. 12 Ye are not straitened in us, but ye are straitened in your own bowels. 13 Now for a recompense in the same, (I speak as unto my children,) be ye also enlarged.

6.11-13 Paul now pleads for heartfelt resolution to those estranged from his leadership. A call is made for love to no longer be held back by the Corinthians but, rather, for them to reciprocate with honesty and affection in return for that of Paul and his aides. As the father figure who planted the seeds of the church in Corinth (1 Cor. 3:6) Paul implores that the people, in kind, have the heart of a child and respond to the tender care.

6.14-18 Be ye not unequally yoked together with unbelievers: for what fellowship hath righteousness with unrighteousness? and what communion hath light with darkness? 15 And what concord hath Christ with Belial? or what part hath he that believeth with an infidel? 16 And what agreement hath the temple of God with idols? for ye are the temple of the living God; as God hath said, I will dwell in them, and walk in them; and I will be their God, and they shall be my people. 17 Wherefore come out from among them, and be ye separate, saith the Lord, and touch not the unclean thing; and I will receive you. 18 And will be a Father unto you, and ye shall be my sons and daughters, saith the Lord Almighty.

6.14-18 In true Levitical fashion, Paul contends that the believers should not "mix" or mingle with non-believers. (Lev. 19:19; Deut. 22:10) The man of God does not intend that Corinthians completely avoid non-believers altogether but urges them that the yoking (binding) be not unequal; the tug of war between the Church and the world will continue until the Lord returns, but what matters is who is pulling harder. God's people are not meant to blend in to the world's darkness but to be candles standing out in His light. (Matt. 5:15) God has never intended that His Church merge, coalesce, integrate, fuse, unite or marry itself to an unGodly world. To the contrary, the Church is to be taken out as a people for His namesake. (1 Sam. 12:22; Acts 15:14) God's law, His Spirit, requirements, and purpose are not in agreement with the ways of man, and the two cannot walk together in this disagreeable state. (Amos 3:3) It was with many other words that Peter, after delivering the plan of salvation, urged a separated, God called people to save themselves "from this untoward generation." (Acts 2:40) As with all parts of God's Message, His promises, and blessings, the results are contingent upon His people holding up their and of the bargain; the Church must come out, it must be separated from the world, and the unclean the must remain untouched in order that God, in His holiness, might be able to receive us. We are to be "Holy" (Hebrew, "qâdôsh," sacred, set aside exclusively for Him) as He is Holy. (Lev. 11:44) (see also Lev. 20:7; Ps. 106:35; Mal. 2:11-15; 1 Pet. 1:15-17)

Chapter 7

7.1 Having therefore these promises, dearly beloved, let us cleanse ourselves from all filthiness of the flesh and spirit, perfecting holiness in the fear of God.

7.1 Continuing on in the concepts set forth in 2. Cor. 6:17, wherein we have the promise of reception at the Master's hand, Paul begins with a charge that God's people avoid all "filthiness" (Greek, "molysmos," stain, immorality) of heart and soul lest we lose that promise which is contingent on our abstinence from all things unholy.

7.2-16 Receive us; we have wronged no man, we have corrupted no man, we have defrauded no man. 3 I speak not this to condemn you: for I have said before, that ye are in our hearts to die and live with you. 4 Great is my boldness of speech toward you, great is my glorying of you: I am filled with comfort, I am exceeding joyful in all our tribulation. 5 For, when we were come into Macedonia, our flesh had no rest, but we were troubled on every side; without were fightings, within were fears. 6 Nevertheless God, that comforteth those that are cast down, comforted us by the coming of Titus; 7 And not by his coming only, but

by the consolation wherewith he was comforted in you, when he told us your earnest desire, your mourning, your fervent mind toward me; so that I rejoiced the more. 8 For though I made you sorry with a letter, I do not repent, though I did repent: for I perceive that the same epistle hath made you sorry, though it were but for a season. 9 Now I rejoice, not that ye were made sorry, but that ye sorrowed to repentance: for ye were made sorry after a godly manner, that ye might receive damage by us in nothing. 10 For godly sorrow worketh repentance to salvation not to be repented of: but the sorrow of the world worketh death.11 For behold this selfsame thing, that ye sorrowed after a godly sort, what carefulness it wrought in you, yea, what clearing of yourselves, yea, what indignation, yea, what fear, yea, what vehement desire, yea, what zeal, yea, what revenge! In all things ye have approved yourselves to be clear in this matter. 12 Wherefore, though I wrote unto you, I did it not for his cause that had done the wrong, nor for his cause that suffered wrong, but that our care for you in the sight of God might appear unto you. 13 Therefore we were comforted in your comfort: yea, and exceedingly the more joyed we for the joy of Titus, because his spirit was refreshed by you all. 14 For if I have boasted any thing to him of you, I am not ashamed; but as we spake all things to you in truth, even so our boasting, which I made before Titus, is found a truth. 15 And his inward affection is more abundant toward you, whilst he remembereth the obedience of you all, how with fear and trembling ye received him. 16 I rejoice therefore that I have confidence in you in all things.

7.2-16 There is no denying that Paul's relationship with the Corinthians had been a mixed one; there were certainly triumphs but, also, several circumstances had brought them both great heartache. Paul had experienced considerable concern over the Corinthians, as well as deep hurt when avoidable situations were nonetheless experienced. Not only this but, as with all relationships, the ebb and flow of emotions and sensibilities does not run in one direction only; Paul's letter had caused the Corinthians a sharp regret. And while Paul had, for a time, regretted sending the letter, as of this moment he is glad because the inner hurt the letter caused had brought about great repentance in the Corinthian church. The sorrow was, in the end, beneficial for the church; those with repentant hearts had changed for the better. The magnitude of their transformation thru repentance was complete, made abundantly clear in the magnificent parlance of 2 Cor. 7:11, one of Paul's most famous writings. In the end, the sorrow each experienced was only momentary, quite apropos his previous discourse on the eternal versus the temporary. Furthermore, the pain had produced joy; when Titus had come Paul felt this and declared "…when he told us your earnest desire…I rejoiced the more." (2 Cor. 7:7). Titus also experienced the same emotions when he learned the sincerity of the Corinthians' faith and witnessed their response to instruction. Ultimately, grave danger had been avoided in Corinth, and the congregation's course was righted. In it all, Paul proved himself worthy of his pastoral role, looking to find the best in Corinth, saying with a full heart, "…great is my glorifying of you…" (2 Cor. 7:4)

Chapter 8

8.1-2 Moreover, brethren, we do you to wit of the grace of God bestowed on the churches of Macedonia; 2 How that in a great trial of affliction the abundance of their joy and their deep poverty abounded unto the riches of their liberality.

8.1-2 Whenever possible, it was Paul's proclivity to inspire and teach by example. He had encouraged the Corinthians, as well as other churches, to imitate his lifestyle of Christ (1 Cor. 4:16; 11:1a; 1 Thes. 1:6; 2 Thes. 3:7-9). These commendations were nor for himself only but included others such as Timothy (1 Cor. 4:17; Phil. 2:19-20), Epaphroditus (Phil. 2:18), and of course, the Lord God (Phil. 2:5; 1 Cor. 11:1b; 1 Thes. 1:6). Here Paul gives two examples of liberal giving to Corinth, the Macedonian churches and Jesus Himself. The Macedonian churches of Philippi, Thessalonica, and Berea had come to know the freedom of Christ through the Word delivered by Paul (Eph. 3:2-12) during his second missionary journey. In Philippi (Acts 16:12-40), Thessalonica (Acts 17:1-9), and Berea (Acts 17:10-15), Paul preached the good news and founded churches. The congregations of these cities often suffered because of their faith (Phil. 1:29-30; 1 Thes. 1:6), but continued faithfully (Phil. 1:5; 1 Thes. 1:7). Philippi had begun it's giving early in the work (Phil. 4:15). Though their material state at times declined, the direction and condition of their spirit was lifted.

8.3-5 For to their power, I bear record, yea, and beyond their power they were willing of themselves; 4 Praying us with much intreaty that we would receive the gift, and take upon us the fellowship of the ministering to the saints. 5 And this they did, not as we hoped, but first gave their own selves to the Lord, and unto us by the will of God.

8.3-5 Paul uses the Macedonian churches as his paradigms of enthusiastic giving; in their desire to be a part of preferring the needs of others they had entreated Paul, on more than one occasion, to be allowed to meet those needs. These congregations had a sincere desire to show their appreciation through giving to "The" Church, not just their own local assembly.

8.6-9 Insomuch that we desired Titus, that as he had begun, so he would also finish in you the same grace also. 7 Therefore, as ye abound in every thing, in faith, and utterance, and knowledge, and in all diligence, and in your love to us, see that ye abound in this grace also. 8 I speak not by commandment, but by occasion of the forwardness of others, and to prove the sincerity of your love. 9 For ye know the grace of our Lord Jesus Christ, that, though he was rich, yet for your sakes he became poor, that ye through his poverty might be rich.

8.6-9 Titus had come by valuable experience in the collection and distribution of free will donations on other occasions (cf. Acts 11:29-30; Gal. 2:1). Paul had, at some point, sent him to begin a collection here in Corinth; now it was time to complete the assignment. Paul writes these words with the sharpness of a double-edged sword. In complimenting the areas in which they have excelled (faith, eloquent speech, knowledge, diligence), he at the same time exhorts them to finish what they have started, not unlike Jesus one day telling a distinguished group of teachers that "ought ye to have done, and not to leave the other undone." (Matthew 23:23) Rather than be dominated by an outside command to give, Paul wishes that the motivation be to prove the condition of their internal devotion to others. Not incidentally, Paul compares their decision to that of the Lord's on our account, leaving the riches of Heaven and choosing instead the poor state of a servant in order to provide our salvation; "So the last shall be first, and the first last…" (Matt. 20:16).

8.10-13 And herein I give my advice: for this is expedient for you, who have begun before, not only to do, but also to be forward a year ago. 11 Now therefore perform the doing of it; that as there was a readiness to will, so there may be a performance also out of that which ye have. 12 For if there be first a willing mind, it is accepted according to that a man hath, and not according to that he hath not. 13 For I mean not that other men be eased, and ye burdened:

8.10-13 Paul's advice (cf. v. 8) was, to finish what you have started (cf. v. 6). Good intentions, even a desire or inclination towards service, are no substitute for action (cf. James 2:15-16). Giving is to be in proportion to what one has been given. The words of Jesus Himself are that basis for Paul's teaching; give, and more will be given, even to a running over and, "…with the same measure that ye mete withal it shall be measured to you again (Luke 6:38).

8.14-15 But by an equality, that now at this time your abundance may be a supply for their want, that their abundance also may be a supply for your want: that there may be equality:15 As it is written, He that had gathered much had nothing over; and he that had gathered little had no lack.

8.14-15 The guiding edict underpinning Paul's teaching in these matters is the idea of "equality" (Greek, "isotes," condition of likeness, proportion of equity) in giving; one is not to be put at a loss for the advancement of another, and vice versa. The foundational truth of the concept comes from the Lord Himself, given to Moses, in His feeding of Israel in the wilderness and here referenced in verse 15; "they gathered every man according to his eating."

8.16-17 But thanks be to God, which put the same earnest care into the heart of Titus for you. 17 For indeed he accepted the exhortation; but being more forward, of his own accord he went unto you.

8.16-17 Not unlike Timothy (Phil. 2:19-20), Titus was veritably interested in the wellbeing of those he served. Paul had requested that Titus assist in the giving project and, by Paul's estimation, Titus had, with earnest care, launched headlong into the work.

8.18-21 And we have sent with him the brother, whose praise is in the gospel throughout all the churches; 19 And not that only, but who was also chosen of the

churches to travel with us with this grace, which is administered by us to the glory of the same Lord, and declaration of your ready mind: 20 Avoiding this, that no man should blame us in this abundance which is administered by us: 21 Providing for honest things, not only in the sight of the Lord, but also in the sight of men.

8.18-21 As a traveling companion on his return to fetch the charity from Corinth, Titus would have with him a minister, most likely from a Macedonian church, who was held in high regard, "praised by all the churches" as preacher of the good news. He would assist in safeguarding Corinth's offering to its final destination in Jerusalem. Paul, ever the provisional planner, had deemed this convoy of evangelists a good idea in order to avoid any further dishonor to their ministry by indictment of avarice or mismanagement (2 Cor. 8:20; cf. 12:17-18).

8.22-24 And we have sent with them our brother, whom we have oftentimes proved diligent in many things, but now much more diligent, upon the great confidence which I have in you. 23 Whether any do enquire of Titus, he is my partner and fellowhelper concerning you: or our brethren be enquired of, they are the messengers of the churches, and the glory of Christ. 24 Wherefore shew ye to them, and before the churches, the proof of your love, and of our boasting on your behalf.

8.22-24 In addition to Titus and the evangelist, a third member (anonymously identified as "our brother") was appointed to join the charity contingent. The particular language of verse 23 seems to indicate he was selected by the Macedonian churches. In this manner, his presence, along with the highly lauded brother of verse 18, served both to help shield Paul and his fellow minsters from any additional accusations of personally profiting from the collection, and also to encourage the Corinthians to join their Macedonian counterparts in giving to the work.

Chapter 9

9.1-5 For as touching the ministering to the saints, it is superfluous for me to write to you: 2 For I know the forwardness of your mind, for which I boast of you to them of Macedonia, that Achaia was ready a year ago; and your zeal hath provoked very many. 3 Yet have I sent the brethren, lest our boasting of you should be in vain in this behalf; that, as I said, ye may be ready: 4 Lest haply if they of Macedonia come with me, and find you unprepared, we (that we say not, ye) should be ashamed in this same confident boasting. 5 Therefore I thought it necessary to exhort the brethren, that they would go before unto you, and make up beforehand your bounty, whereof ye had notice before, that the same might be ready, as a matter of bounty, and not as of covetousness.

9.1-5 The Corinthians' past had, on some level, given Paul a bit of pause in his confidence of their following through. He continues, and with no small amount of adamancy, in imploring the church to make good on their promises. Paul reminds them that, a year ago, it was their initial aspiration and penchant towards the Jerusalem offering which had spurred the other churches to take action. Moreover, Paul had made much to do over the Corinthians' notions to the Macedonians and he was anxious, if not a bit fearful, that when the delegation arrived Corinth might not have it's offering ready. Corinth was motivated to help (cf. 8:4), a fact, which Paul had communicated to the Macedonians a year previous, and this had, in effect, been the tipping point to bring the Macedonians to action. The distinction between the Corinthians and Macedonians, though, lay in their respective persistence to see the project plan through to fulfillment. While slow to begin, the Macedonians had finished strong. Quick to enlist, Corinth lacked the determination to win the battle of the flesh; they needed resolve to fight a good fight, finish the course, and keep the faith of their promises (2. Tim. 4:7).

9.6-11 But this I say, He which soweth sparingly shall reap also sparingly; and he which soweth bountifully shall reap also bountifully. 7 Every man according as he purposeth in his heart, so let him give; not grudgingly, or of necessity: for God loveth a cheerful giver. 8 And God is able to make all grace abound toward you; that ye, always having all sufficiency in all things, may abound to every good work: 9 (As it is written, He hath dispersed abroad; he hath given to the poor: his righteousness remaineth for ever. 10 Now he that ministereth seed to the sower both minister bread for your food, and multiply your seed sown, and increase the fruits of your righteousness;) 11 Being enriched in every thing to all bountifulness, which causeth through us thanksgiving to God.

9.6-11 Paul now invokes the time-tested adage based on the truth of the Book; "you reap what you sow." The principle is not only Biblically sound but is echoed in the planting and harvesting seasons of the natural world. When seed is scattered, the sower is increased; the one who waters will be watered, but the one who holds back the corn will be cursed (Prov. 11:24-26) For a truth, whether in the realm of the natural or the spiritual, the size of a harvest is dictated by the scope of the sowing. It is the giver's sincerity (not reluctance), purposed decision (not obligation or constraint), and willingness (not hesitancy) that bestows the Godly designation of a joyous giver (cf. 9:7). Understandably then, this type of church contributor Paul is talking about is the one who is "cheerful" (Greek, "hilaros," propitious or merry); not surprisingly it is from this Greek word that we derive our own English "hilarious." The sheer, lighthearted exuberance wherewith the Apostolic giver bestows upon the church invokes a riotous smile and buyout glee; this type of giving is infectious, providing an extreme amusement for both the one giving and the one receiving. The magnitude of shedding the inborn human tendency towards selfish protection of personal property, above all other concerns, is the definition of hilarity, of high Spirited levity. Provision is guaranteed for the child of God for, we being no different than the bird which cannot store up in barns, the Lord sees each and furnishes exactly what is needed (Matt. 6:26). The quotation of verse 9 is a reminder that the saint who "hath dispersed abroad" and "hath given to the poor" will have their good deeds remembered in eternity (Psalm 112:9) On the opposite end of this spectrum is that person who is much concerned with accumulation and gain; we would do well to remember it was this "barn builder mentality" which merited the Lord's appellation of fool (Luke 12:18-21). It is God alone who provides the seed, the bread and increase, and the cheerful giver will have their giving multiplied (Matt.

14:13-21); they will, in every way, be enriched by God so that the generosity may continue.

9.12-15 For the administration of this service not only supplieth the want of the saints, but is abundant also by many thanksgivings unto God; 13 Whiles by the experiment of this ministration they glorify God for your professed subjection unto the gospel of Christ, and for your liberal distribution unto them, and unto all men; 14 And by their prayer for you, which long after you for the exceeding grace of God in you. 15 Thanks be unto God for his unspeakable gift.

9.12-15 Much is accomplished in this "administration" (Greek, "diakonia," attendance as a servant)(cf. 9:12) of ministry to another. The "experiment" (Greek, "dokime," test, proof) (cf. 9:13) will both satisfy the needs of brothers and sisters in Christ and, at the same time, bring glory to God for those blessed will offer Him the thanks for supplying all their request. The feeling of this gift, both for the giver and the one receiving, is "unspeakable" (Greek "anekdiegetos," not fully expounded), having no words adequate for its description.

Chapter 10

10.1-2 Now I Paul myself beseech you by the meekness and gentleness of Christ, who in presence am base among you, but being absent am bold toward you: 2 But I beseech you, that I may not be bold when I am present with that confidence, wherewith I think to be bold against some, which think of us as if we walked according to the flesh.

10.1-2 Perhaps remembering the Proverb instructing us to have all facts in order before judgment is meted out (Prov. 18:13) Paul was reluctant to take stern action; it was his back up plan, however, the situation and opposition at Corinth had made confrontation his last and only viable option. To his credit, Paul was patterning his behavior after the Lord's. It was Christ's meekness (Matt. 11:29) that was His greatest strength and it was that which enabled Him to placidly accept the transgressions done against Himself (e.g., Matt. 27:12-14). The Lord's meekness was the living embodiment of the strength that arises in loving others more than self. It was this driving force that penned Paul's urgent words, a last request that the hearts of any opposers be righted before his arrival so that uncomfortable and undesirable confrontation was not necessary.

10.3-5 For though we walk in the flesh, we do not war after the flesh: 4 (For the weapons of our warfare are not carnal, but mighty through God to the pulling down of strong holds;) 5 Casting down imaginations, and every high thing that exalteth itself against the knowledge of God, and bringing into captivity every thought to the obedience of Christ;

10.3-5 What follows Paul's plea for reconciliation is a reminder that the Lord does not gauge the strengths and prowess of His Apostolic Church by the same standards as the world's. Paul had discounted the confidence in fleshly things to the church at Philippi (Phil. 3:4-8) and Corinth was no different; it would not be with impressive credentials (1. Cor. 1:26) or with eloquent speech (1 Cor. 2:1) that the battle for souls was waged. The weapons of the saint of God are not those of the world, rather, they are the only and reliable Spiritual weapons we have, namely, the Word of God and prayer (Eph. 6:17-18). The one seeming wise to himself God will capture in his own craftiness (Job 5:13) and, to the Lord, all his thoughts are nothing but vanity (Psa. 94:11).

10.6-8 And having in a readiness to revenge all disobedience, when your obedience is fulfilled. 7 Do ye look on things after the outward appearance? if any man trust to himself that he is Christ's, let him of himself think this again, that, as he is Christ's, even so are we Christ's. 8 For though I should boast somewhat more of our authority, which the Lord hath given us for edification, and not for your destruction, I should not be ashamed:

10.6-8 There were at least two goals now present in

Paul's mind. Firstly, Corinth needed to display their obedience to Christ by openly accepting and supporting the authority God had granted to the leadership of the church there, principally, Paul and his ministerial support. Secondly, after the church's obedience was "fulfilled" (Greek, "pleroo," supplied, finished, verified) (cf.6). Paul was then ready to dispense judgment, as necessary, to the remaining, destructive opposition. It was imperative that the church understand there is no hierarchal stratification of God's acceptance. In the Lord's eyes, there is no middle ground; one is either for the church or against it (Luke 9:49-50). Those that would be for the church would also be for its ministry and in favor of righting the wrongs present; unity was of the highest importance. With respect to their ability to succeed and move forward, Paul was careful to explain that the seriousness of fully supporting the ministry could not be overstated.

10.9-11 That I may not seem as if I would terrify you by letters. 10 For his letters, say they, are weighty and powerful; but his bodily presence is weak, and his speech contemptible. 11 Let such an one think this, that, such as we are in word by letters when we are absent, such will we be also in deed when we are present.

10.9-11 Paul was the first to admit to his own superficial un-impressiveness (cf.1). However, his explanation makes it clear that he does not desire to frighten those who believe in him with the force of the letter. At the same time, to those who would say he was weak and ineffectual in person, Paul vows clearly that these matters will be, once and for all, laid to rest with their coming arrival.

10.12 For we dare not make ourselves of the number, or compare ourselves with some that commend themselves: but they measuring themselves by themselves, and comparing themselves among themselves, are not wise.

10.12 In his previous letter Paul had made the case that God has eternally disproved and invalidated any wisdom that man believes he has on his own merit (1 Cor. 1:20). Nevertheless, the unruly faction within the church touted their own self-proclaimed merits among themselves; Paul and his ministerial brethren refused to be counted among such a number and rejected the flesh's occasion to glory in self (Jer.9:23).

10.13-15 But we will not boast of things without our measure, but according to the measure of the rule which God hath distributed to us, a measure to reach even unto you. 14 For we stretch not ourselves beyond our measure, as though we reached not unto you: for we are come as far as to you also in preaching the gospel of Christ: 15 Not boasting of things without our measure, that is, of other men's labours; but having hope, when your faith is increased, that we shall be enlarged by you according to our rule abundantly,

10.13-15 In a direct assault on the false prophets' footing, Paul daringly makes known that he and his fellow ministers have stayed within the bounds of the authority God had granted. It was Paul, not these wolves in sheep clothing, whom God had called to go unto the Gentiles (Gal. 2:8), and he was the first to reach Corinth with the good news (cf. 14). Moreover, Paul and his associates will not lay claim to the work of another as, apparently, these false prophets had done.

10.16-18 To preach the gospel in the regions beyond you, and not to boast in another man's line of things made ready to our hand. 17 But he that glorieth, let him glory in the Lord. 18 For not he that commendeth himself is approved, but whom the Lord commendeth.

10.16-18 A charge is now laid directly into the hands of Corinth; Paul wishes that they grow and mature as Christians so that he may continue his work in regions beyond Corinth. If others were to experience the power of the Gospel it would be exclusively because the Corinthians grew sufficiently so that all of his time was not monopolized in the one geographic. Always an apt student of the prophets, Paul here invokes Jeremiah (Jer. 9:24) to put it clearly, and succinctly, that if glory is to be conferred, it belongs exclusively to God. It will not be the self righteous ones approving themselves who will be found worthy, but only the one of whom the Lord boasts will be approved. Paul understood the Lord's teaching, that self commendation and the praise of men count for nothing, whether it is in giving, praying, fasting, or any endeavor of the church (Matt. 6:2, 6, 16). All that is done is to be done for the Lord alone (Col. 3:23) and all in the name of Jesus (Col. 3:17).

Chapter 11

11.1-2 Would to God ye could bear with me a little in my folly: and indeed bear with me. 2 For I am jealous over you with godly jealousy: for I have espoused you to one husband, that I may present you as a chaste virgin to Christ.

11.1-2 With heartfelt sentiment Paul unashamedly admits to "folly" (Greek, "aphrosyne," foolishness, recklessness) with regard to his feelings over Corinth. He is "jealous" (Greek, "zelos," fiercely zealous) over them to the point of doing whatever it would take to ensure their faithfulness, as the bride of Christ, to the bridegroom. He would gladly be called reckless, for his love and care for them is of such degree that one viewing from on the outside might find it verging on the foolish.

11.3-4 But I fear, lest by any means, as the serpent beguiled Eve through his subtilty, so your minds should be corrupted from the simplicity that is in Christ. 4 For if he that cometh preacheth another Jesus, whom we have not preached, or if ye receive another spirit, which ye have not received, or another gospel, which ye have not accepted, ye might well bear with him.

11.3-4 As Paul had elsewhere compared Jesus with Adam (Rom. 5:14; 1 Cor. 15:21-22, 45), Paul here compares the Corinthian church to Eve in the garden, and he is afraid that, like Eve, Corinth will fall to the same temptation, a perversion of the Gospel. Rather than resist (James 4:7; 1 Peter 5:9) Paul insists that the Corinthians to seem to be convinced and enamored with every new "wind of doctrine" (Eph. 4:14), an observation not unlike the one he had made at Galatia (Gal. 1:7).

11.5-6 For I suppose I was not a whit behind the very chiefest apostles. 6 But though I be rude in speech, yet not in knowledge; but we have been throughly made manifest among you in all things.

11.5-6 There was never a time when Paul claimed to be the most eloquent, sophisticated, cosmopolitan speaker. Indeed, quite to the contrary, Paul seemed to revel in the fact that souls were saved specifically in the absence of any such human quality of "enticing words of man's wisdom"; he was not to be personally lauded for his life was nothing but a "demonstration of the Spirit and of power." (1 Cor. 2:4) But where Paul lacked in the haute couture style of many of his contemporaries, he more than made up for it with abounding knowledge (cf. 6). He did not consider himself any less important to God's work than the "chiefest apostles" and had remarked to the Galatians that Peter, James, and John had themselves given him the "right hands of fellowship" (Gal. 2:9)

11.7-12 Have I committed an offence in abasing myself that ye might be exalted, because I have preached to you the gospel of God freely? 8 I robbed other churches, taking wages of them, to do you service. 9 And when I

was present with you, and wanted, I was chargeable to no man: for that which was lacking to me the brethren which came from Macedonia supplied: and in all things I have kept myself from being burdensome unto you, and so will I keep myself. 10 As the truth of Christ is in me, no man shall stop me of this boasting in the regions of Achaia. 11 Wherefore? because I love you not? God knoweth. 12 But what I do, that I will do, that I may cut off occasion from them which desire occasion; that wherein they glory, they may be found even as we.

11.7-12 Not willing to leave any stone unturned, Paul begins now to address another of the false prophets' failings that, namely, how that they had received remunerations for supposed work done. Jesus Himself had instructed evangelists to received shelter and provision from those to whom they ministered (Luke 9:3-4; 10:4-7). Unfortunately, this practice had also apparently been exploited by the false apostles in Corinth. The difference in Paul and his fellow ministers (e.g., Barnabas, 1 Cor. 9:6) was that they had repeatedly, and often, supported themselves in the absence of any compensation from the church (cf. 1 Cor. 4:12; 1 Thes. 2:9; 2 Thes. 3:8). While there were times when Paul received unsought aide from churches(e.g., the Philippian church in Macedonia; Phil. 4:15-16) he did so with reserve (cf. Phil. 4:10-13),and here calls what he did "robbery" (2 Cor. 11:8), taking from a poor congregation in order to continue his work in Corinth. Paul truly did not want to be a burden anywhere he was.

11.13-16 For such are false apostles, deceitful workers, transforming themselves into the apostles of Christ. 14 And no marvel; for Satan himself is transformed

into an angel of light. 15 Therefore it is no great thing if his ministers also be transformed as the ministers of righteousness; whose end shall be according to their works. 16 I say again, let no man think me a fool; if otherwise, yet as a fool receive me, that I may boast myself a little.

11.13-16 If Paul had held anything back up to this point, it seems that here his floodgate of pent up frustration was released and, with reckless abandon, begins to "tell it like it is." Without any hesitation Paul calls the charlatans what they are, "false prophets" (Greek, "*pseudapostolos*," pretend preachers), "transforming" (Greek, "*metaschematizo*," change the outward form, disguise) themselves into emissaries from God when, in fact, they were messengers of Satan masquerading about as angels of light. Their description is akin to the warning of Jesus Himself regarding ravening wolves in sheep clothing (Matt. 7:15) and the identification of hypocrites who, like whitewashed tombs, have delivered righteousness externally but contain nothing but death inwardly (cf. Matt. 23:27-28).

11.17-21 That which I speak, I speak it not after the Lord, but as it were foolishly, in this confidence of boasting. 18 Seeing that many glory after the flesh, I will glory also. 19 For ye suffer fools gladly, seeing ye yourselves are wise. 20 For ye suffer, if a man bring you into bondage, if a man devour you, if a man take of you, if a man exalt himself, if a man smite you on the face. 21 I speak as concerning reproach, as though we had been weak. Howbeit whereinsoever any is bold, (I speak foolishly,) I am bold also.

11.17-21 Fighting fire with fire, Paul answers the

foolish Corinthians according to their folly (Prov. 26:5). Previously asked to "put up with" a bit of foolishness (2 Cor. 11:1), the Corinthians now are now awarded with more. This was not Paul's preference, taking the low road, but by necessity because Corinth had tolerated too much for too long. They had, without hesitation apparently, received those false teachers because of the latter's external qualifications and self-aggrandizement. What ensues is Paul's "contest of folly." In 2 Corinthians Paul frequently speaks of boasting, and not out of pride but in an attempt to validate his apostleship. Paul openly admits this is not the Lord's way, but Paul feels he has no over recourse to make his case. The ironies and comparisons Paul makes border on sarcasm with a sting is tempered only by a loving desire to see their eyes opened. The Corinthians, naively thinking themselves wise, have put up with fools, a grossly foolish thing to do! Were it not for his correction they would fall prey to allowing these frauds to "devour" (Greek, "katesthio," to eat down, consume, as in a parasite) them completely; interestingly this devouring is the same designation the Lord applied to the practices of the pharisees (Mark 12:40). Paul had been too weak for that, not willing to go to that extreme; if he had been anything at all, he was their servant.

11.22-27 Are they Hebrews? so am I. Are they Israelites? so am I. Are they the seed of Abraham? so am I. 23 Are they ministers of Christ? (I speak as a fool) I am more; in labours more abundant, in stripes above measure, in prisons more frequent, in deaths oft. 24 Of the Jews five times received I forty stripes save one. 25 Thrice was I beaten with rods, once was I stoned, thrice I suffered shipwreck, a night and a day I have been in the deep; 26 In journeyings often, in

perils of waters, in perils of robbers, in perils by mine own countrymen, in perils by the heathen, in perils in the city, in perils in the wilderness, in perils in the sea, in perils among false brethren; 27 In weariness and painfulness, in watchings often, in hunger and thirst, in fastings often, in cold and nakedness.

11.22-27 Paul was now begins comparing the external qualifications apparently believed by the Corinthians and the false apostles to be matters of great importance. It is generally understood that the questions asked and answered by Paul describe himself and the false apostles. Paul was a Hebrew, an Israelite, tracing his lineage through the tribe of Benjamin (Phil. 3:5). He was a descendent of Abraham's, circumcised on the eighth day (Phil. 3:5; cf. Gen. 17:9-14); more importantly, Paul was Abraham's descendant by faith (cf. Rom. 4:16). If these human standards were their measuring rubric then Paul measured up perfectly (cf. Phil. 3:4-6). Paul had been a servant in the most intense, extreme fulfillment of the definition possible. In scope of ministry and experience no apostle could equal Paul's service record. The most remarkable reality of these testimonials is that he does not focus on the high marks, his triumphs in the Church, but rather on difficulties and defeats. He does not mention moments on top of the mountain, as in the miracles of Ephesus (Acts 19:11), but in stead chooses to draw attention to his pains, perils, and sufferings. The list is like a crash course of his book of Acts ministry chronicling events that would have crushed a lesser man long before. Herein, most likely, lies the reason for his focus on the calamity and strife; the true test of a loving pastor's care and calling comes not when he is living in the overflow of blessing, but battling through in the greatest trials of his life while never loving the flock any less. In this, Paul stands shoulders above the rest; he is without compare in dogged, ferocious determination to live and die for Christ (Phil. 1:21; Rom. 14:8).

11.28-33 Beside those things that are without, that which cometh upon me daily, the care of all the churches. 29 Who is weak, and I am not weak? who is offended, and I burn not? 30 If I must needs glory, I will glory of the things which concern mine infirmities. 31 The God and Father of our Lord Jesus Christ, which is blessed for evermore, knoweth that I lie not. 32 In Damascus the governor under Aretas the king kept the city of the damascenes with a garrison, desirous to apprehend me: 33 And through a window in a basket was I let down by the wall, and escaped his hands.

11.28-33 In spite of all the turmoil, it is the care of the churches, which dominates his mind day to day. Paul feels their pains, he hurts with them, is injured with them in failings, and if any glorying is to be done, it will be to glorify in the sharing of these sufferings which unveils human weakness. In these things a lasting commitment shines through, even when it means being lowered in a basket to escape a city in order to continue preaching the Gospel (Acts 9:19-25).

Chapter 12

12.1-5 It is not expedient for me doubtless to glory. I will come to visions and revelations of the Lord. 2 I knew a man in Christ above fourteen years ago, (whether in the body, I cannot tell; or whether out of the body, I cannot tell: God knoweth;) such an one caught up to the third heaven. 3 And I knew such a man, (whether in the body, or out of the body, I cannot tell: God knoweth;) 4 How that he was caught up into paradise, and heard unspeakable words, which it is not lawful for a man to utter. 5 Of such an one will I glory: yet of myself I will not glory, but in mine infirmities.

12.1-5 Paul now redirects to another line of comparison concerning visions and revelations. Like his outward credentials Paul saw this mention of spiritual experience to be an exercise in futility, but did it, nonetheless, in the hopes quieting his critics and reaching Corinth. The vision had occurred 14 years earlier, probably sometime around 42-44 AD before Paul's missionary journeys reported in Acts. Paul was taken up to the third heaven, the dwelling place of the Lord and the saints, which Jesus called paradise (Luke 23:43; cf. Rev. 2:7) and what he heard he was forbidden to communicate. This vision, in all likelihood, had contributed greatly to Paul's strong belief that the things we go through "worketh for us a far more exceeding and eternal weight of glory" (2 Cor. 4:17). But even in this, Paul refuses to elaborate deciding that, instead, it is better to focus on his areas of weakness.

12.6 For though I would desire to glory, I shall not be a fool; for I will say the truth: but now I forbear, lest any man should think of me above that which he seeth me to be, or that he heareth of me.

12.6 Paul is candid in saying that if he were to focus or rely on boasting of such things that at least he could do so truthfully, implying that the claims of other men in Corinth were suspect. But what mattered to Paul was not his achievements but God's work through him and the gospel that he preached.

12.7-10 And lest I should be exalted above measure through the abundance of the revelations, there was given to me a thorn in the flesh, the messenger of Satan to buffet me, lest I should be exalted above measure. 8 For this thing I besought the Lord thrice, that it might depart from me. 9 And he said unto me, My grace is sufficient for thee: for my strength is made perfect in weakness. Most gladly therefore will I rather glory in my infirmities, that the power of Christ may rest upon me. 10 Therefore I take pleasure in infirmities, in reproaches, in necessities, in persecutions, in distresses for Christ's sake: for when I am weak, then am I strong.

12.7-10 What follows has been considered one of Paul's greatest literary achievements and, indeed, one of his most oft quoted and discussed pieces of writing. Lest he fall to self-exaltation, and in what has brought many a saint of God a measure of solace through their own trial, Paul admits to the constant reminder of weakness in the form of a God given "thorn" (Greek, "*skolops*," point, annoyance, disability). Innumerable explanations have been offered throughout the generations concerning the nature of this "thorn" in the flesh; they range from incessant temptation, tireless opposition, chronic sickness (such as ophthalmia, malaria, migraine headaches, and epilepsy), to a speech impediment. While no one can say for sure what his was, it is clearly something that caused Paul no small amount of suffering and anxiety. It's personal level of magnitude for Paul is echoed in the fact that Paul had repeatedly petitioned God for its removal (2 Cor. 12:8). In the heat of this trying flame Paul learned the lesson which predominates all other teaching to the Corinthians in this letter: God's power and ability is most extravagantly exhibited against the backdrop of human weaknesses. In this manner, God alone is praised. Adeptly connecting with countless believers to follow him, Paul instructs how that, at times, rather than removing the thorn God will grant grace to endure it. This grace is "sufficient" (Greek, "arkeo," enough, satisfactory) to keep the saint through the trial. What was, at first, difficult for Paul to accept and endure came to be a point of Godly pride and pleasure in that he understood God's power was being manifest as he weathered the storm. While the difficulty sometimes overshadowed Paul, it made Christ that much more visible. Only when Paul felt utterly alone and at the end of himself Christ be formed in him (Gal. 4:19). Only when he became weak could the Lord be strong.

12.11-21 I am become a fool in glorying; ye have compelled me: for I ought to have been commended of you: for in nothing am I behind the very chiefest apostles, though I be nothing. 12 Truly the signs of an apostle were wrought among you in all patience, in signs, and wonders, and mighty deeds. 13 For what is it wherein ye were inferior to other churches, except it be that I myself was not burdensome to you? forgive me this wrong. 14 Behold, the third time I am ready to come to you; and I will not be burdensome to you: for I seek not yours but you: for the children ought not to lay up for the parents, but the parents for the children. 15 And I will very gladly spend and be spent for you; though the more abundantly I love you, the less I be loved. 16 But be it so, I did not burden you: nevertheless, being crafty, I caught you with guile. 17 Did I make a gain of you by any of them whom I sent unto you? 18 I desired Titus, and with him I sent a brother. Did Titus make a gain of you? walked we not in the same spirit? walked we not in the same steps? 19 Again, think ye that we excuse ourselves unto you? we speak before God in Christ: but we do all things, dearly beloved, for your edifying. 20 For I fear, lest, when I come, I shall not find you such as I would, and that I shall be found unto you such as ye would not: lest there be debates, envyings, wraths, strifes, backbitings, whisperings, swellings, tumults: 21 And lest, when I come again, my God will humble me among you, and that I shall bewail many which have sinned already, and have not repented of the uncleanness and fornication and lasciviousness which they have committed.

12.11-21 Now having caused Paul to play the fool, Corinth is asked to see reason, to clearly look back at

Paul's track record, the miracles, signs, wonders, and remember clearly hat in all he did, Paul never took from them but only gave of himself. In coming to them the third time, again, Paul would gladly receive absolutely nothing from their hand if they would but listen, be challenged, and change. As the father figure of the Corinthian church he proclaims it is not for the child to provide for the parent but, rather, for he to give all to them. He would spend himself, use himself up for their sake, though, at times, it seems as if the more he does the less he is appreciated. While some would contend for his defense in the matter of being blameless before them, a faction still existed which had suspected trickery and guile in his motives. In one last, desperate attempt, Paul reminds them of his own visits, and that of Titus and their fellow workers, how that nothing was asked, expected, or extorted from the Corinthians but, in all things, they acted as servants of Christ. Paul is candid with his trepidation over the coming visit. He fears there will be confrontation when he arrives, the need to reprimand old and undefeated sins, and that he will be grieved to find the Roman Corinthian standards of "uncleanness" (Greek, "akatharsia," impurity), fornication, and "lasciviousness" (Greek, "aselgeia," filthiness, licentiousness) still being flown high.

Chapter 13

13.1-3 This is the third time I am coming to you. In the mouth of two or three witnesses shall every word be established. 2 I told you before, and foretell you, as if I were present, the second time; and being absent now I write to them which heretofore have sinned, and to all other, that, if I come again, I will not spare: 3 Since ye seek a proof of Christ speaking in me, which to you-ward is not weak, but is mighty in you.

13.1-3 Without question, and as the words of this letter attest, Paul's second visit to Corinth (2 Cor. 2:1) had been a humbling one (12:21). Several factors were pivotal in this, not the least of which were the offenses and disobedience against his authority (2 Cor. 2:5-11), but more hurtful to Paul still were the many living in sin (2 Cor. 12:21). Paul had forewarned them of the repercussions of sin in that visit, and this letter served as not so gentle a reminder that there would be discipline for the unrepentant. In the manner of the Lord Jesus (Matt. 18:16), Paul enacts the principle of Deuteronomy 19:15 in reference to having two or three witnesses for any and all claims. While some still demanded proof of his ministry's legitimacy, Paul makes it clear that the proof will come in a manner that they would do well to avoid (1 Cor. 5:5). Though the apostle himself was admittedly weak, the Lord whom he served was not (2 Cor. 10:4).

13.4 For though he was crucified through weakness, yet he liveth by the power of God. For we also are weak in him, but we shall live with him by the power of God toward you.

13.4 With the ultimatum set forth Corinth would be wise to make ready by the humbling of certain among them. While the Lord Jesus had chosen the path of service and weakness, His resurrection showcased only the slightest hint of all His glorious, untapped power at the ready (Eph. 1:19-21). In like manner, Paul and his apostolic, ministerial cohort might have been weak in their own right, but once the Holy Ghost started to use them they would become the unstoppable force of Heaven.

13.5-7 Examine yourselves, whether ye be in the faith; prove your own selves. Know ye not your own selves, how that Jesus Christ is in you, except ye be reprobates? 6 But I trust that ye shall know that we are not reprobates. 7 Now I pray to God that ye do no evil; not that we should appear approved, but that ye should do that which is honest, though we be as reprobates.

13.5-7 Throughout the course of this letter the majority of scrutiny had been focused on Paul, his ministry, and that of his brethren. Now, with the authority of closing argument before a Heavenly Judiciary, Paul hands the mirror to the Corinthians and challenges them to reflect. In that image they would soon find flaws, which needed correcting, and would then see the fault did not lay, nor had it ever, with Paul. With much grace the man of God proclaims that he would prefer that no pastoral authority be exercised; it would be his will that all necessary changes would be made before his arrival so that there would not be occasion for correction.

13.8-10 For we can do nothing against the truth, but for the truth. 9 For we are glad, when we are weak, and ye are strong: and this also we wish, even your perfection. 10 Therefore I write these things being absent, lest being present I should use sharpness, according to the power which the Lord hath given me to edification, and not to destruction.

13.8-10 Paul was eager to be merciful, lenient, and forgiving with the Corinthians. He, above all people, knew that there was no point in trying to strand against truth; the knee bending, blinding power of his Damascus road experience had taught him that (Acts 9:1-6). More concerned about the church's welfare than anything (cf. Phil. 2:20-21) Paul would gladly be weak for their sakes. Having spent himself completely, giving all for their benefit, his strength would lie in seeing them mature. The authority given him would be best served in a constructive fashion rather than in tearing down.

13.11-14 Finally, brethren, farewell. Be perfect, be of good comfort, be of one mind, live in peace; and the God of love and peace shall be with you. 12 Greet one another with an holy kiss. 13 All the saints salute you. 14 The grace of the Lord Jesus Christ, and the love of God, and the communion of the Holy Ghost, be with you all. Amen.

13.11-14 The last call of Paul's letter is one urging unity, maturity, joy, and peace. If they could but reach that state, God's grace would help them weather all storms. Much like what Paul had told the Ephesians (Eph. 4:16), Corinth needed Holy Ghost power to give them binding ties of agreement in Jesus' name. For this Corinthian congregation and for all the churches Paul would minister too, his message of distinction would be to rally the people to harmony (Phil. 2:20-21), to be of one mind and one accord; indeed, these were the conditions necessary for the Spirit to fall in the beginning (Acts 2:1-4).

www.ingramcontent.com/pod-product-compliance
Lightning Source LLC
Chambersburg PA
CBHW040417100526
44588CB00022B/2860